GYPSIES

GYPSIES

by HOWARD GREENFELD

Crown Publishers, Inc., New York

10 9 8 7 6 5 4 3 2 1

The text of this book is set in 12 point Palatino. The illustrations are black and white photographs, reproduced in halftone.

LIBRARY OF CONGRESS CATALOGING IN PUBLICATION DATA
Greenfeld, Howard.   Gypsies.
Bibliography: p. 105 Includes index. SUMMARY: An account of the Gypsy way of life, including its origins, history, traditions, customs, occupations, and the changes that modern living has occasioned.   1.Gypsies—Juvenile literature. [1.Gypsies] I.Title.
DX118.G68 1977   301.45′19′1497   77-23746   ISBN 0-517-52842-8

Also by Howard Greenfeld

Books: From Writer to Reader

They Came to Paris

F. Scott Fitzgerald

Gertrude Stein: A Biography

Contents

GYPSIES

Introduction

THERE ARE BETWEEN FIVE AND TEN MILLION GYPSIES wandering the world today; more accurate figures are impossible because they are forever on the move and rarely included in a census. They are true nomads—that is, they travel from place to place, never wanting to settle down, never wanting to join an established, stable community. They have their own customs and traditions, many of which have been influenced by the non-Gypsies among whom they have traveled, but what makes them unique and what they all have in common is their nomadism.

They live—always temporarily—at the edge of cities, at the edge of our society. They are, for the most part, hated and feared, all too often blamed for crimes of which they are not guilty, such as kidnapping babies, sorcery, and, in the past, even cannibalism. They have often been officially

1

discriminated against and have been almost always shunned by the non-Gypsy society of which they themselves, ironically, want no part. They are outsiders, and most of them want to remain so. They have in some way created and maintained the alternative society that so many people seek, and they are proud of it.

There are many different tribes of Gypsies, and scholars differ among themselves as to the various classifications. There are the Kalderash, the Lowara, the Gitanos, the Manush, and the Bohemians, to name only a few. The general name for all true Gypsies is Rom, which in the language of the Gypsies means man as well as Gypsy, and it is with the Rom that this book will deal. Though the names of the various Gypsy tribes differ, the roots of the Rom are the same. Each tribe might have developed different habits and customs, but all Gypsies have a common tradition and way of life that can be portrayed.

An accurate portrayal is, unfortunately, a difficult task, complicated by the Gypsies themselves. Most Gypsies are illiterate and therefore have no written history. In addition, they have no sense of the past and are not interested in recounting or even knowing about it. And even if they did, these extraordinarily secretive people would reveal nothing to the Gaje (as they call the non-Gypsy), whom they dislike and mistrust, and with whom they rarely have any real contact. Their traditions and customs and ceremonies—and even their true names—are only reluctantly disclosed to non-Gypsies, and even then there are reasons to doubt their accuracy. It has been said that if you ask twenty Gypsies the same question, you will get twenty different answers; and that if you put the same question to one Gypsy twenty times, you will also get

2

twenty different answers. There have been occasional accounts of Gypsy life by non-Gypsies who have been permitted to live and travel with the Gypsies, but there have been far too few of these.

What are Gypsies, then? For many people, just the word "Gypsy" conjures up the picture of dirty women in long skirts, apparently sickly babies in their arms, begging for money or asking to read palms. For others, they are petty swindlers who rent storefronts and deceive a gullible public.

According to their detractors, Gypsies must be lazy because they don't work. They find them dark and ugly, so they assume they don't wash. They say they drink far too much and are out of control after a few drinks. Gypsies are accused of being sexually promiscuous, their women ready to seduce non-Gypsy men, their men always on the lookout for innocent non-Gypsy women. They are said to possess evil powers of magic and to be capable of casting malevolent spells. Above all, Gypsies are charged with cheating and stealing from the Gaje whenever possible.

They are, according to these people, a diseased element, extraneous to our society.

There is, however, another—and equally one-sided—picture of the Gypsy, and this is a romantic one. According to this point of view, they are a beautiful, colorfully dressed people—proud and independent, gay and life-loving and passionate. They are carefree and enjoy the simple pleasures of life: the sun, the moon, and the stars. These nature lovers, too, have created a music and dance that throb with passion and joy. The women in their colorful long skirts are irresistibly seductive and exciting; the dark-faced, high-cheekboned men, so proud of bearing, are symbols of wild, uninhibited virility.

These notions have, for centuries, been encouraged by romantic writers and painters all over the world, and they are as untrue as those others that show the Gypsies to be a totally immoral and disreputable people.

This book is an attempt to balance these two opposing points of view by giving an honest account of the Gypsy way of life. In learning of their origins, history, and traditions, their customs, occupations, and the changes that modern living has brought about, it is possible to reach at least a partial comprehension of this greatly misunderstood group.

I

Origins: Myths and Reality

THE GYPSIES ORIGINALLY CAME FROM INDIA. THIS SIMPLE fact was unknown until the nineteenth century, several hundred years after their first appearance in Europe. Europeans must have wondered where these strangers who infiltrated their continent came from, but not enough to investigate the matter methodically. In fact, the people among whom they traveled showed a surprising lack of curiosity about their origins, satisfying themselves with a number of vague and fundamentally unconvincing myths to explain the roots of these wandering people they called Gypsies. Perhaps they didn't feel the Gypsies were worthy of scientific investigation; perhaps, too, Europeans preferred to attribute a mysterious romantic past to these bands of wanderers.

As for the Gypsies themselves, they were of little help.

They were truly indifferent to their own past, and it better suited their purposes to encourage fanciful, imaginative explanations of their origins. If they said these origins were biblical and therefore Christian—and many proclaimed this in spite of the fact that they practiced magic, read palms, and committed numerous petty thefts—they could more easily gain the sympathy of the people and the officials of the towns and cities they visited. If, instead, these roots were tinged with mystery, this would enhance their qualifications for fortune-telling, their most common way of making a living, and give them a certain diabolical power over the natives.

Many of the myths of biblical origin were very popular. According to some, the Gypsies were descended from Noah; according to others, they were the true descendants of Abraham and Sarah. Their endless wandering, some people believed, was their punishment for being among those who refused help to Joseph and Mary on their flight into Egypt. There was even a myth to explain their not working for a living: since they were a result of Adam's first marriage—prior to the one with Eve—they were not concerned with original sin and thus did not have to earn their bread as decreed by the Bible.

Many biblical citations, too, were used to explain the plight of the Gypsies. Their nomadism is explained by Ezekiel—*I shall scatter the Egyptians among the nations*—and in the Book of Genesis—*A fugitive and a vagabond thou shalt be in the earth*. There are other citations from Genesis: *Father of such as dwell in tents* predicts their way of living, and *Father of all such as handle the harp and organ* could account for their interest in music.

One of the most widespread legends concerning the

A Gypsy family outside their wagon.

Gypsies' need to wander was based on the story of the Crucifixion. It seems, from this legend, that many people were asked to forge the nails of the Cross, but all refused when they heard the purpose for which the nails were to be used. Finally, some Gypsy smiths agreed to make them, and because of this, Gypsies were condemned to wander forever.

Many speculations on their origins were not based on biblical sources. They themselves often said they had fled from Egypt and supported this by the use of fanciful titles, such as "Duke of Egypt." Another popular story told that during the crossing of the Red Sea, when Pharaoh's troops were trapped in the waters, a young couple miraculously escaped, becoming the Adam and Eve of the Gypsies.

The Gypsies, too, were thought to be of Babylonian descent, or of Nubian, or of Abyssinian, or even descendants of the Celtic Druids. No explanation of their origins seemed impossible, and a particularly romantic version stated that they were the survivors of the mysterious people who inhabited the legendary island of Atlantis, which was totally destroyed by an earthquake.

Sometimes, the Gypsies' choice of occupations was supposed to provide clues to their origins. For example, because of their skills at fortune-telling, they were reputed to be the descendants of the Euxians, neighbors of the Persians, who in ancient times were known for their success in predicting the future. More plausible than this, however, were those hypotheses that linked the Gypsies' origins with their skill as metalworkers—an art they practiced in each country that they visited. This relationship of the Gypsy to the forge was given serious attention by a well-known French scholar, Paul Bataillard, in the nineteenth century, who concluded that the Gypsies were descended from a people known as Sintians, who lived during the time of Homer. The modern Gypsies had two things in common with these Sintians: they were both races of highly skilled metalworkers, and they both spoke a strange, incomprehensible language. According to Bataillard's theory, for which there was no substantial proof, the Gypsies whom everyone held in such contempt would have been the people who had first introduced

A metalworker in Paris.

metallurgy to the continent of Europe, and had in this way made a major contribution to Western civilization.

All of these myths or theories are colorful, but none is based on fact, and the truth about the origins of the Gypsies did not begin to emerge until the latter part of the eighteenth century—and then it happened almost by accident. In 1763, a Viennese newspaper reported that a Hungarian theological student named Stefan Valyi, working at the University of Leiden in the Netherlands, had met three Indian students from the Malabar coast whose language struck him as remarkably similar to that spoken by the Gypsies he had known in Hungary. Intrigued by a possible relationship between the two, Valyi, upon his return to Hungary, showed the Gypsies he knew a number of words that had been used by the Indian students. The Gypsies had no difficulty understanding the words shown to them.

It was this chance meeting that provided the first clue as to the real origins of the Gypsies. Valyi's lead was followed up by other scholars who, too, found great similarities in the two languages and, based on their studies, speculated that the first homeland of the Gypsies must have been India.

In the middle of the nineteenth century, more thorough investigations were conducted. Scholars carefully analyzed every aspect of the language spoken by the Gypsies—called Romany—and it became increasingly clear that it was an Indian language of Aryan origin, connected with Sanskrit. More than half of the basic Romany vocabulary was related to languages spoken in northern India.

Further research concluded that these Gypsies were directly descended from two Indian groups, the Luri and the

Dom. The Luri were a tribe of wandering minstrels who showed no interest in settling down and were accused of petty thievery wherever they went. The Dom, too, came from northern India and had been known for centuries as nomads. The word "Dom" in Sanskrit designates people of low caste who make their living singing and dancing, just as many Gypsies do.

Scholars have to this day been unable to reach agreement as to why the Gypsies left India for Europe. But just as the study of language enabled them to determine the origins of the Gypsies, it has enabled them to trace the paths these wanderers took from the time they left India, in about the year A.D. 1000. This has been established through a study of foreign words that found their way into the language spoken by the Gypsies. The number of these foreign words adopted by the Gypsies would correspond to the length of time they spent in various countries.

From India, it seems that they went to Afghanistan and then on to Iran—these Persian-speaking regions left their mark on the Gypsies' Sanskrit-based language. From there, it is probable that some groups went to the Arabic-speaking lands of Syria and North Africa, while others spent a great deal of time in the countries where Greek was spoken. Then, before reaching western Europe, they must have crossed the entire Balkan peninsula, where their language was enriched by words from the Bulgarians, Rumanians, and Slavs.

II

The Gypsies Arrive in Europe

THE PEOPLE OF WESTERN EUROPE FIRST SAW THE GYPSIES in the early decades of the fifteenth century; they had never seen people like that before. Traveling in small groups, never more than a hundred at a time, their appearance and behavior aroused curiosity and mistrust wherever they went.

These foreigners were, for the most part, dark-skinned, with raven-black hair: the men, though poorly dressed, looked proud and almost arrogant; the women seemed mysterious, their long, tattered skirts betraying a poverty that was in sharp contrast to the golden jewelry so many of them wore. They spoke in an incomprehensible language and called themselves by names never before heard in the countries through which they passed. They did not seem at all interested in settling down, in taking jobs, in

12

becoming a part of the lands they visited.

From the few existing documents of the time, it seems that these strange people were first officially noticed in Germany. They arrived there in long caravans; some of the men were on horses, while others were on foot, and their picturesque wagons were filled with baggage as well as with women and children. The Germans welcomed them warmly; these dark-skinned people seemed peaceful, they claimed to be good Christians, and they brought with them letters of protection from various highly respected leaders, among them Sigismund, king of Hungary. All these impressive letters asked that kindness and generosity be shown to these strangers, and the Germans obediently complied.

Similar letters were presented to the citizens when, shortly afterward, the Gypsies were first reported in France, Belgium, the Netherlands, and Denmark. Again, they were greeted hospitably, were given provisions, and granted the right to camp.

In 1422, they were reported making their first appearance in Bologna, Italy. Led by a chief who called himself Duke Michael of Egypt, about one hundred men, women, and children settled near one of the gates to the city. Before very long, they were not—for good reasons—popular with the citizenry. It became known that the wife of Duke Michael was a fortune-teller, and soon many curious women of the town went to visit her and seek her advice and predictions. During these visits, many women had their fortunes told—and they also had their purses robbed. Others had pieces of their dresses cut off. In addition to this, houses and shops were robbed, and throughout all of Bologna there were reports of petty thievery.

The people of Bologna found these strange people not only dishonest, but physically repulsive. "The ugliest brood ever seen in this country. They are thin and black, and they eat like swine" is what a chronicle of the time had to say about them.

Finally, an official decree was issued stating that anyone who went to see them or did any business with them would be fined and excommunicated. No longer able to function in the city, the Gypsies left Bologna—they had stayed only three weeks.

Their next stop was Rome, where they sought and, it seems, received an audience with Pope Martin V. There is some evidence that the Pope provided them with an all-important letter of safe-conduct.

For the next five years, there are no written accounts of the travels of these Gypsies. Where they went remains a mystery. Then, on August 17, 1427, they appeared in Paris, and the report of their arrival and short stay in the French capital (which was then a part of England) is the most colorful and detailed of any of these contemporary chronicles.

At first, there were only twelve of them: a duke, an earl, and ten other men—all on horseback. They announced that they came from Lower Egypt and that they were good Christians. They were, they said, penitents who had traveled a long and hard road to Rome to seek forgiveness from Pope Martin V for having once strayed from Christianity. After they had confessed their sins to the Pope, the Pope said they must, as a penance, wander for seven years without sleeping in a bed. To aid them in their travels, the Pope had given them letters asking bishops and prelates along the way to show them kindness.

According to this story, which they recounted in Paris—they had told a similar tale in Bologna—they had already been traveling for five years. The rest of their group—another hundred or so—joined the original twelve after a short time, but, instead of being allowed to enter the city, they were forced to stop at the gate of La Chapelle.

Their arrival caused enormous excitement. Mobs of Parisians came to see them, to stare in curiosity and in horror, as is clear from this contemporary account:

> The men were very dark, their hair was fuzzy; the women the ugliest and swarthiest ever seen; all had their faces covered with sores, and their black hair looked like a horse's tail. They were dressed in old, coarse blankets, fastened to their shoulders by pieces of cloth or cord; their only undergarment was an old smock or a chemise.
>
> In short, they were the most wretched creatures seen coming to France within the memory of man.

As they did in Bologna, these "wretched creatures" read palms and stole as they did so. Their wild and often dire predictions disrupted lives and spread fear and panic among those who had listened to them.

When words of their activities finally reached the Archbishop of Paris, he went to visit their encampment and, through an aide, he decreed that not only the fortune-tellers but all those who went to them for consultations would be excommunicated. In a short time, the Gypsies left Paris, much as they had left Bologna, leaving an irate citizenry behind them.

In spite of these early setbacks, the number of Gypsies

French Gypsies.

traveling in all parts of the continent of Europe increased dramatically within a short time, though they were little more than a minor curiosity at first. Europeans in the fifteenth and sixteenth centuries had far more important concerns. It was a period of enormous social and economic turmoil for the entire continent, and the arrival of small, scattered groups of dark-skinned nomads was hardly noticed.

Yet they were there, and as time went by, their presence could not be ignored. Europeans saw them only as a rootless people, wanting neither homes nor jobs. Their morals and their way of life contrasted too greatly with that of the non-Gypsy. They defied or simply ignored the basic values of the people among whom they traveled. They were an irritant as well as a social, cultural, and economic threat.

III

Centuries of Persecution

EUROPEANS DECIDED THAT THE ONLY WAY TO DEAL WITH THE Gypsies was to make them disappear. There were three basic ways of accomplishing this—expulsion, repression, and assimilation. In some cases, where one way failed, another was adopted.

The easiest and most direct method was simply not allowing them into a country or getting rid of them physically if they did manage to get in. A good example of this was Scandinavia. The king of Denmark, in 1589, decreed that any leader of a Gypsy band found on Danish soil was to be sentenced to death. In the seventeenth century, it was declared that any vessel bringing in Gypsies would be confiscated. From that time on—and until 1849—any Gypsy found in Denmark was subject to deportation. Until that time, too, Gypsy hunts were organized with

18

honors and rewards to those who captured a Gypsy.

Norway, too, confiscated any vessel that brought Gypsies to Norwegian soil, under the terms of a law that was not liberalized until the nineteenth century, when Norway passed a law allowing Gypsies to remain in the country if they abandoned their nomadic ways. Even then, Norwegians found the Gypsy way of life unsanitary, and, because of that, felt justified in taking Gypsy children away from their parents.

Sweden probably had the harshest laws of all. Gypsies were not allowed to enter the country; those who managed to do so were immediately expelled; and those who failed to leave were brutally attacked or hanged. But there was a problem—all Gypsies who managed to escape to neighboring Finland were driven back to Sweden, since Finland didn't want them either.

France, too, enacted a series of expulsion laws beginning in 1510. Throughout the sixteenth century any Gypsies caught in the country were flogged "because of their alleged religion and frauds." They were to be driven away by "fire and sword" as well. In the following century, Gypsy women who were captured had their heads shaved and were sent to workhouses; the men were put into chains in galleys forever.

For the English, the Gypsies were sorcerers, thieves, and cheats; they even caused disease in cattle. In the sixteenth century, they were ordered to leave or be imprisoned because they had committed "many and haynous Felonyes." In 1544, many of these Gypsies were forcibly deported, but the deportation backfired. They were sent to France, and the French simply sent them back across the Channel to England, a repetition of what had happened in Scandinavia. Signs dotted the English countryside, telling the Gypsies that they must leave England, but they were illiterate and could not read the signs. Nonetheless, those who remained were given forty days to leave. Failure to do so meant death. In spite of this, many hid in the countryside, aided by non-Gypsies who found their way of life attractive. Then, in 1562, all English men and women who showed any sympathy with the Gypsies became subject to punishment. The Gypsy way of life was in itself a crime, and those who kept company with or in any way imitated Gypsies were guilty of this crime.

Expulsion of Gypsies also served economic purposes at times, since some European countries found it useful to people their colonies with cheap sources of labor. For this reason, the English sent many of their Gypsies to Barbados, Australia, and to parts of North America; the French planned to send many of their Gypsies to Louisiana in the early nineteenth century (a plan that had to be abandoned when Louisiana was sold to the United States); the Portuguese sent hundreds of their Gypsies to Brazil; and the Spanish deported many to their South American colonies.

Repressive laws, rather than outright expulsion, have also been common. Nomadism was banned in Spain, and the speaking of Romany was not allowed. Gypsies had to abandon their traditional clothing and were forbidden from possessing horses or working as smiths. In a further effort to eliminate Gypsies, no marriage was permitted between them, nor were they allowed to gather in large groups. At one time, Gypsies who neither conformed to Spanish ways nor left the country were made slaves.

Slavery, too, was a solution to the "Gypsy problem" in other countries. Because of a shortage of workers in Wallachia and Moldavia (now Rumania), Gypsies were forced into serfdom for a period of time. They were owned by local rulers, and some were even owned by the government. The church not only condoned this practice but bought some Gypsy slaves for its own purposes. This inhuman practice continued until the middle of the nineteenth century.

In Hungary, too, the Gypsies were taken into slavery during the fifteenth century. Once freed, things were not much better, and a number of restrictive measures were taken against them, including a 1740 law which stated that no Gypsy could work in metal outside of his tent. This law was obviously aimed at thwarting any attempt the Gypsies might make to compete against native metalworkers.

Other examples of cruel treatment abound. Switzerland allowed Gypsy hunts in the sixteenth century, as did Holland in the eighteenth. The Gypsies were treated like wild animals, objects of a chase. The central European lands of Moravia and Bohemia, which are now part of Czechoslovakia, took novel measures against the Gypsies. In Moravia, it was permissible to cut off the left ear of all Gypsy women; in Bohemia, removal of the right ear was legal.

When neither expulsion nor repression failed to solve the problem of the Gypsies, a more subtle—and apparently more humane—approach was tried, and that was assimilation. By giving them incentives to settle down, to abandon their Gypsy ways and behave like the rest of the world, the Gypsies would become, over a period of time, invisible.

21

A few examples of this will suffice. In 1761, the queen of Hungary, realizing that the Gypsies were determined to stay in the country, decided to turn these Gypsies into what she called "New Hungarians." They were generously given tools and seed and animals and were to be transformed into farmers, in spite of the fact that they had never shown any interest in the land. Their language was outlawed, and they were no longer permitted to trade horses or to sleep in tents. The queen's son and successor carried on and implemented his mother's policies. Nomadic communities were forced to settle, children were required to attend school and go to church, and adolescent Gypsies were taken from their families and made to learn trades. Even Gypsy music could not be played except on special holidays. All these measures failed, and by the nineteenth century the Gypsies had gained a certain amount of freedom to be Gypsies.

By the end of the eighteenth century, Spain, too, realized that expulsion or repression was not the answer to the "Gypsy problem." It seemed wiser to encourage these people to give up their way of life and to become integrated with the Spanish people. A law was passed that called "Rules for Repressing and Chastising the vagrant mode of life, and other excesses, of those who are called Gypsies." The way of life was to be repressed and not the people. Gypsies could follow any career of their choosing, any profession that was open to Spaniards— but only if they renounced their own way of life.

The same was true in France, when the French realized that the Gypsies were stubbornly determined to remain in their country. Laws were enacted that encouraged the Gypsies to find jobs and settle, giving up their traditional ways and eventually integrating into French society, but the Gypsies remained Gypsies.

Expulsion, repression, attempts at assimilation—all these represent one attitude toward the Gypsies, and that attitude is hostility. This fundamental hostility has remained unchanged, reaching its most tragic limits in Hitler's Germany before and during World War II.

The Gypsies presented a special problem for the German dictator. The cruel racist policies he directed against the Jews were based on the latter being non-Aryans; Gypsies, being one of the oldest Aryan groups in Europe, could obviously not fit into this category. At first, the Hitler regime tried to force German scholars to deny the truth, and to state that Gypsies were not Aryans. However, many scholars refused to go along with Hitler's demands—a refusal that often led to their own imprisonment.

After a while, this tactic was abandoned, and more convincing pretexts were invented for doing away with the Gypsies. They were not Nordic, they were "asocial," they were "subhuman beings" and members of a "lower race."

Because of this, beginning in 1937, the Gypsies were rounded up and put into concentration camps, which were more politely called "resident camps." The Gypsies to be caged included not only those found in Germany itself, but also any found in the countries invaded and conquered by Hitler's troops.

Being a Gypsy meant being diseased, so these prisoners were sterilized to prevent them from spreading this disease by reproduction. They were forced to work and to live in inhuman conditions—as long as they were allowed to live.

The fate of the Gypsies during World War II paralleled the tragic fate of the Jews, who were also imprisoned and exterminated. The names of the notorious concentration camps are the same—Dachau, Belsen, Buchenwald—and they evoke memories of the same nightmarish experiences as those the Jews suffered. They were tortured, they were used for inhuman scientific experiments, and they were put to death in the infamous gas chambers. One of the worst of the camps, Auschwitz, held sixteen thousand Gypsies at one point.

By August 1944, only four thousand Gypsies remained in Auschwitz. After a visit by one of Hitler's deputies, Heinrich Himmler, these last imprisoned nomads were led to the gas chambers and destroyed. It is estimated that approximately one quarter of a million Gypsies were murdered from 1939 to the end of World War II.

IV

Organized Nomadism

THE GYPSIES HAVE ALWAYS LIVED IN A HOSTILE WORLD, among people who wanted to eliminate them, and it seems almost miraculous that they have been able to survive. In addition, Gypsy life has always been governed by nature, which can be equally cruel and unpredictable. Gypsy camps have always been in danger of being broken up by an angry populace or by the police in the lands they have visited when social tensions become too great. However, they are an ingenious people, accustomed to hardship, and usually able to solve this problem by simply moving on to another location.

The restrictions set by the seasons and the weather cannot, in this way, be escaped. Their activities are regulated not only by sunrise and sunset, but by climatic conditions. Their movements are determined by the seasons. They begin to travel in the spring, and they temporarily settle in the winter when travel conditions are usually unfavorable. During the cold winter months, Gypsies encamp in locations where they can be protected as much as possible from the snow and cold. Preferably, too, this location is on the outskirts of a town, so that the women can go to the town to beg and to tell fortunes, and the men can sell or trade horses there. Life during the winter is difficult; the hours are short and the weather is hostile to outdoor living.

A Gypsy camp in Hungary.

In the springtime, with the advent of warmer weather, the Gypsies return to the road, awakened and renewed. Spring is the time for large gatherings and festivals, for horse fairs and for pilgrimages to such places as Saintes-Maries-de-la-Mer in the south of France, or Padua in Italy, or Appleby in England. These large and colorful assemblies of Gypsies are an annual opportunity to meet friends and relatives and to exchange news and information. Once they end, each group takes off again to begin its travels, usually following the same routes taken the previous year.

In the past, Gypsies have traveled in caravans, putting their tents and their few personal possessions into colorfully painted horse-drawn wagons and carts. In modern times, the wooden wagons have been replaced by mechanized means—large cars, trailers, and campers.

The choice of a campsite—winter or summer—has always been dictated by several factors. Proximity to grazing lands was once of great importance, as was nearness to a running stream or other sources of water. It has been important to find a location where the earth was solid so that their vehicles would not sink into the ground.

It has always been best to encamp in an isolated area, as far as possible from public view. The Gypsies want their privacy and do not like being observed by local residents. Also, if they are remote from main roads, there is less risk of being chased away by local authorities. An out-of-the-way site could also prevent their being caught and punished for misdeeds committed in their previous stopping place.

Given these extremely harsh conditions, at the mercy of hostile peoples and unpredictable weather conditions, it

Gypsies traveling by wagon.

can only be wondered how the Gypsies have managed to survive. The answer lies not only in their remarkable toughness and determination, but also in their tightly controlled social organization, which stresses strong family and community ties, and in their strict code of traditional laws. To a non-Gypsy their wandering existence might seem aimless—and their nomadism might well have been an insurmountable barrier to a regulated life—but the Gypsies, within their own framework, have been proven to be a remarkably well-organized people.

The Gypsy community that travels together is known as

28

a *kumpania*—it can consist of as few as ten separate families or of as many as several hundred separate families. The ties of a *kumpania* are residential, in that they share the same camping area; and they are economic, in that they share the resources of any given area and monopolize the work that is available to them in that area. The *kumpania* is most often a temporary alliance, based on convenience, and, whenever necessary, it can be easily broken up or modified.

The same is not true of alliances that are based on blood relationships. Though these family groups might not live together, or be part of the same *kumpania*, the family is a close unit, characterized by a great sense of loyalty. Only the smallest group, consisting of grandparents, children, and grandchildren, generally live together in one household, sharing the tasks to be performed; while the larger group, which is called the *familia*, might be divided into many areas. This *familia* consists of three or four generations, and it is usually led by the eldest member of the group.

An even larger unit of Gypsies is known as a *vitsa*. This is made up of a number of *familia;* some of these are large and some are relatively small, but all members of a *vitsa* are descended from one ancestor. This relationship might well go back several generations, but it is a close one. Though members of one *vitsa* might live very far from each other, they manage to keep in touch regularly.

Obviously, communications among these nomadic groups without fixed homes or schedules are very difficult, but they keep informed of each other's movements and whereabouts by ingenious means, which have enabled them to band together for special occasions, such as

*The annual Gypsy gathering at Saintes-Maries-de-la-Mer
in the south of France.*

weddings and funerals, or in times of need. The traditional system of communication, used for centuries, is called the *vurma*, and it is unique among Gypsies. This *vurma* is a trail of messages in code, left along roadsides, which will lead to Gypsy encampments or further contact points. These messages can be in the form of twigs, bones, bits of glass, colored threads, or scraps of other materials. The Gypsies know just where to look for these objects—they are placed above the sight line of a non-Gypsy passerby (who wouldn't recognize them, in any case) and are for this reason unlikely to be removed.

Nowadays, with greater distances between them, the Gypsies utilize modern means of communication. They establish contact points—these might be cafés, bars, public offices, stores, or remote inns—at which they receive mail or telephone calls at appointed hours. Whenever an emergency arises, Gypsies have an almost uncanny ability to locate one another, and they unfailingly respond to the needs of other members of their *familia* or *vitsa*.

These binding family and community ties have certainly strengthened the Gypsies in their struggle to survive, but an even greater force has been their system of morality and justice, which has acted as the major source of discipline, so essential in what otherwise could have become a chaotic, unlawful existence.

There is no such thing as Gypsy royalty. No king or duke makes proclamations of law. Gypsies did use imaginative titles of nobility when they first came to Europe, but these were meant to impress their hosts. Since that time, many journalists have found it colorful to write of Gypsy kings or queens, and some Gypsies—seeking a romantic image—have encouraged this. However, the fact is that each community is ruled by a man who is chosen not because he is part of any royal family but for his age, experience, and wisdom. The leader of a Gypsy community is a man who inspires respect by his strength and intelligence, a man who by his own life sets an example for the other Gypsies. He settles minor disputes on the basis of his mature judgment, and his decisions are followed by other members of the community. However, if the matter to be settled is a serious one—theft, adultery, acts of physical violence, or complicated disputes between two individuals or two families—a court is convened. This court, the most important moral force in Gypsy life, is called the *kris*.

Calling together a *kris* is an event of utmost importance in Gypsy life. The members of the court, especially convened for the occasion, are the most respected and wisest men available at the time; no women are ever included. Of these members, one—most often the eldest—is chosen to preside at the hearings.

The *kris* can last for several days, and each case is carefully deliberated. The judges wear no special clothing, but there is an air of great dignity and solemnity throughout the proceedings. Witnesses are called, and the accused or the two parties in a dispute swear to tell the truth—sometimes before a candle, or a piece of iron, and sometimes in the name of the dead or in the name of one's son.

After all the evidence has been heard, the court makes its decision based on strict traditions and moral standards. These have never been written down or codified—they have been passed along for generations by word of mouth—but this fact makes the decisions nonetheless binding. The *kris* is the ultimate power in Gypsy society,

A Gypsy caravan.

to be both feared and obeyed. For the Gypsy, the decisions of the *kris* carry far more weight than do the judgments of any civil court, to which they might be subject on some occasions. Indeed, vindication by a non-Gypsy civil court does not erase a previous conviction by the *kris* in the mind of the Gypsy.

If, at the end of a trial, the defendant is found to be innocent, there is great joy and relief in the community. A banquet of rehabilitation will be held, and the former defendant has the right to propose the first toast. If, on the other hand, the defendant is found guilty, any number of different penalties might be invoked. These range from the largely symbolic one of having to pay all court expenses—including food and drink for the judges—to the most serious of all, banishment from the community of Gypsies.

There are no jails or executioners in a Gypsy community, but it is impossible to think of a more severe punishment for a Gypsy than banishment from his own community. It is, in effect, a sentence of social death. This banishment is achieved by declaring the offender *marime*, a term that means socially rejected.

The offender cannot have any social contact with other members of the tribe. The simple pleasures of Gypsy life —eating together, camaraderie—are forbidden, and the guilty party is condemned to live in the dreaded world of the non-Gypsy. In most cases, not only the offender, but his or her own family as well, is declared *marime*. This harsh punishment is a great deterrent to crime within the Gypsy community. It can last for days or years; it involves permanent loss of status and respect even when the guilty party has been reinstated.

36

V

Traditional Occupations

NOMADISM HAS INFLUENCED EVERY ASPECT OF GYPSY LIFE; and it has been—along with their refusal to depend on the non-Gypsy for a steady income—the determining factor in the kinds of occupations they have chosen. Jobs undertaken by members of a stable, settled community would be impossible for them, and they have traditionally sought work that could be done by a people on the move, work that required little—and light—equipment, as well as work that did not call for year-round attention. Because of this, agriculture, which would have necessitated permanent residence, had never interested them until recent times, when Gypsies began to take on occasional summer jobs as farm workers.

Because they have shown themselves to be remarkably adaptable to changing conditions in different countries, it

Weaving a basket.

is impossible to do more than generalize about the traditional occupations of the Gypsies. However, there have been two conditions that a job must meet before it will be of interest to a Gypsy. One is that it must allow the Gypsy to be free to travel; and the other is that it should call for as little steady, direct contact with the non-Gypsy as possible.

In general, Gypsy occupations are divided by sex: men are the artisans while women offer services, such as fortune-telling, and sell what the men produce. It is the women who bring in the money, and the women who are largely responsible for spending it and giving it to the men when they need it.

Gypsy vendors have always been a common sight near any Gypsy encampment. Because their movements and travels are always uncertain, they are unable to build up a steady clientele in any one place. For this reason, they are forced to try to sell their wares to passersby, or by going from house to house. The articles they sell are of little value: minor objects such as baskets, brooms, rakes, wooden spoons, and combs. Because these products are easily obtainable from regular, local suppliers, and the ones made by Gypsies are often of not very good quality, their selling is almost the equivalent of begging. There are certainly some good craftsmen among the Gypsies, but for the most part people buy from them out of pity—or, even more frequently, merely to get rid of them.

One area in which male Gypsies have traditionally excelled is that of metalwork; they were known as metalworkers from the beginning of their history. This form of work fits in well with the image of the diabolical Gypsy; there is, after all, something mysterious about the work of

An artisan continues a century-old occupation.

the smith, who bends metal to his will with the aid of fire. The art of the forge is an ancient one, making use of the fundamental elements of water and fire, and the Gypsy seems to have learned this extraordinary art while in India, where it was considered a "disgraceful occupation," not worthy of the higher castes.

40

Traditional Occupations

The Gypsies have been experts in all forms of metal-work—whether it be as tinsmiths, coppersmiths, or silversmiths. They have made nails, tools, kitchen equipment, and arms. They have been skilled at plating objects with tin, or embossing and engraving pieces of jewelry. Some have been masters at making false coins, and others—especially in Hungary and Rumania—have been gold washers, collecting gold deposits from the bottoms of rivers.

Coppersmiths.

Gypsies have not only been master smiths, but they have also shown great ingenuity in devising relatively light equipment, such as forges and hammers, which are necessary to their work and which can be more easily transported than can the generally massive tools used by smiths.

Just as male Gypsies have always shown an affinity for working with metal, they have long been renowned as horse-dealers. Because horses were essential for transportation in the early days of migration, their care and treatment were of great importance to the Gypsies. The Gypsy, in addition, feels great affection for this animal, which has played such an important part in his life. No one is more capable of capturing wild horses, breeding them, and then transforming them into workable animals than the Gypsy. The skills of these people in curing the illnesses of horses that others less knowledgeable would discard as hopeless have served them for centuries. Often they would trade a good horse for an apparently less healthy one, collecting needed money for the difference. By caring for these sick horses and putting them into good condition, they were later able to sell them for a far higher price than the original one paid.

Skilled dealers as well, the Gypsies made a specialty of attending horse fairs; these were major occasions in their lives, occasions for pleasure as well as business. They were adept at pointing out the advantages of their own horses—which had been carefully taken care of before the fairs—and concealing or minimizing their defects. By the same token, they knew how to emphasize the disadvantages of those horses they were interested in buying, thereby bringing down their prices.

The horse has always been an important economic factor in the life of the Gypsy, and the Gypsies' understanding of this animal has been widely recognized—so much so that, for many years, it was common among the country people of eastern Europe to bypass the village veterinarian and go to a Gypsy to cure an ailing horse.

The Gypsies are, as a group, animal lovers, and next to the horse, the animal they have shown greatest interest in is the bear. Because of this, Gypsies traditionally have found work as bear leaders—that is, men who could train bears for entertainment purposes. It was not an uncom-

Gypsies today train horses to be circus performers.

Yovanovich, a modern bear trainer, entertaining in Paris.

mon sight for many years, especially in Europe, to see a Gypsy leading a dancing bear through the streets and collecting coins from amused passersby. Even today, some of these bear leaders are found in eastern Europe.

The occupation for which the Gypsy has always been most famous is a woman's activity—fortune-telling. Indeed, the classical and most familiar image of the Gypsy woman is that of the fortune-teller.

There are three main reasons that fortune-telling has appealed to the Gypsies. First of all, it gave them an aura of mystery and of magic; in this way it served as a means of self-protection, building up a fear of curses or spells in

44

the non-Gypsy. Quite often, too, since it was the one means of "intimate" contact with the non-Gypsy world, fortune-tellers were useful in learning of the social, political, and economic climate of a region they might contemplate visiting for a length of time. Their clients often took them into their confidence, revealing facets of local conditions the Gypsies would otherwise be unable to judge. Finally, of course, fortune-telling was a relatively simple way of earning money from and winning a degree of power over a gullible public.

Gypsies have been adept at every kind of prediction. They have read tea leaves, seen visions in crystal balls, and analyzed the future from reading cards. Above all, they have been expert in palmistry, judging a person's fate, character, and aptitudes from the shape of hands and fingers and the designs of lines in the hand.

Though they claim that their great powers of prediction come from heaven, the real skill of fortune-tellers lies in their great shrewdness in judging human character and in exploiting human weaknesses. To please their believing clients, they most often predict a favorable future: the lonely girl will find a rich and handsome husband; the man will find a rich and beautiful bride—and they will have a long and happy marriage. To strike a degree of fear and awe, there will be mysterious warnings of perils which might well be avoided by rather costly preventatives—provided, of course, by the Gypsy.

The Gypsy fortune-teller is a good judge of human nature; she knows that most people remember what comes true and forget what does not. She knows, too, that she is capable of adding an exotic, exciting element to the life of an insecure non-Gypsy, and she feels—or pretends to

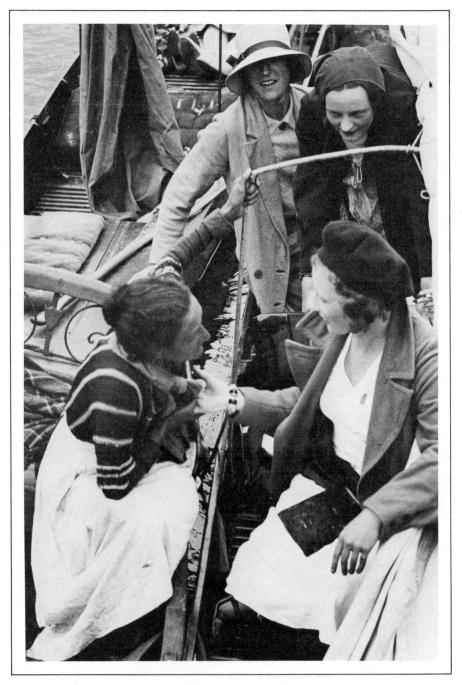

A Gypsy tells a young woman her fortune.

feel—that she is doing a service by, in some way, acting as a confidante to these lonely people. She is playing on their fears and superstitions, but only on those of the non-Gypsy, for Gypsies—though a superstitious people themselves—never practice their skills as fortune-tellers on other Gypsies.

Although fortune-telling is basically a hoax, Gypsy musicians and dancers have made a genuine contribution to the non-Gypsy world. Gypsy soloists and orchestras have entertained non-Gypsies since they first came to Europe. Documents show that they were favored as court musicians in Hungary in the fifteenth century, and throughout Europe for several centuries since then. The instruments preferred by Gypsy musicians have been the guitar, the lute, percussions (especially cymbals), the cello, and the violin. The violin has best been able to express a wide range of emotions for the Gypsies. Though their orchestras have included the clarinet, they seldom use brass or wind instruments. Their music is gay and bright, and it can also be moving and soulful. Since the large majority of Gypsies have been unable to read music, their skill at improvisation is all the more remarkable.

Apart from their undisputed role as excellent performers, their actual contribution to the composition of music has been disputed. Composers as far apart as Franz Liszt and Béla Bartók have acknowledged the marked Gypsy influence on the colorful, rhythmic music of Hungary. However, it seems clear that what the Gypsies did was borrow from the music of the countries they passed through in their travels, adding to it their own flavor, rather than creating a wholly new music of their own.

The same is true of the so-called Gypsy music of Spain,

which has enjoyed enormous popularity. When we note the great differences between Spanish Gypsy music and Hungarian Gypsy music, it becomes clear that neither is Gypsy music as such, but both are brilliant and inventive adaptations of the local music, to which the Gypsies have made certain original contributions.

This is also the case with so-called Gypsy dance, which is largely the flamenco, a dance that originated in Andalusia and which has become famous throughout the world. This stirring dance, performed by proud men and seductive women stamping their feet and snapping their fingers with awesome intensity and passion, is largely associated with the Gypsies; some of the finest flamenco dancers have certainly been Gypsies. Nonetheless, as with so much Spanish music, what the Gypsies did was to adapt and even popularize a dramatic and exciting dance form that is traditionally Spanish and not Gypsy.

If occupations are defined as activities by which a people make a living, it is at this point that one of the most common and least commendable ways that Gypsies survive economically must be mentioned: petty thievery and begging. These activities are not to be excused or condoned; they are justifiably abhorred by non-Gypsy society. However, they should be understood within the context of Gypsy customs and morals as well as the Gypsies' possibilities for obtaining their basic necessities.

Fundamental to Gypsy thought is complete contempt for the non-Gypsy, for whom they feel no love or affection, no real ties at all. Because of this, stealing from the Gaje is not considered a crime; it is an achievement, a proof of the superior cleverness of the Gypsy. So, by the same token, is begging. The Gypsy beggar—always a

A Gypsy fortune-teller.

A Gypsy dancer.

woman—deliberately looks dirty. She scratches and coughs and does her best to be repulsive, so that the Gaje will give her money just to get rid of her.

The Gypsies believe that stealing from or begging from the non-Gypsy is justifiable for other reasons. First of all, since Gypsies have no real sense of private property or possessions, outside their own communities everything that belongs to the world of the non-Gypsy is, in effect, for public use. This explains why, when Gypsies steal or beg, they feel no guilt for what non-Gypsies consider to be immoral acts or punishable crimes.

Robberies committed by Gypsies, and they are traditionally petty ones, have been based on need. The Gypsies see nothing wrong in picking grass for their horses, stealing wood for their fires, or plundering fruits and chickens for their dinners. Robberies are committed not for gain but out of necessity. Gypsies point out that they do not rob banks for large amounts of money, nor do they kidnap children for ransom, as the non-Gypsies do. They do not steal from each other—theft within Gypsy society is a serious crime—so they are not natural thieves. Barred from stable occupations by their nomadism as well as by the restrictions of the societies among which they travel, petty thievery and begging have seemed to them natural solutions to their problems of day-to-day living.

VI

Personal Habits and Beliefs

THE PERSONAL HABITS AND BELIEFS OF GYPSIES ARE greatly influenced by their nomadic way of life. Religion is one example. Most probably because they have not settled among any peoples and have not built stable communities of their own with places in which to worship, they cannot be said to have a religion of their own. Though they have, for practical purposes, adopted the religions of those with whom they have come into contact, formal religion has been replaced by faith in magic, in omens both good and bad, in powerful curses, and in miraculous cures. This body of superstitions, some of which are no stranger than the superstitions of non-Gypsies, varies among different Gypsy groups, but it is to some extent a factor in the lives of all of them.

Good luck charms, amulets, and talismans are common—they are carried to achieve love, wealth, or happiness, and to prevent misfortune or heal sickness. Some Gypsies carry bread in their pockets as protection against bad luck or witches or ghosts. Others believe that coconuts bring good luck, while still others wear ornaments made of seashells or of hand-shaped objects to ward off evil. Horseshoes are considered good luck by Gypsies just as they are by non-Gypsies.

Since Gypsies feel that illness is an unnatural condition, there are many supernatural ways in which they believe disease can be prevented or cured. To prevent diseases of childhood, some children carry around their necks a black bag containing fragments of a bat; others wear coral beads, strung with red cotton or wool, as protection.

One method of lowering a fever has been to go to a forest and shake a young tree; the fever is in this way transferred from the sick person's body to the tree. Another method to bring down fever has been to drink powdered frogs' lungs and livers, dissolved in spirits, to the accompaniment of a chant. Carrying a mole's foot is a cure for rheumatism, and carrying a hedgehog's foot can prevent a toothache. Other medicines include the fat of a bear, the flesh of a snake, or the brain of a bird. In addition, any number of herbs are used for the prevention or cure of various diseases.

Fundamental to the Gypsy way of life is a belief in invisible spirits, in ghosts, and in vampires, who haunt the fields and the forests and the rivers. These must all be carefully guarded against, or combatted by the use of spells and charms. These are, as we will learn, above all associated with the rites relating to dying and the dead.

Gypsy clothing, too, is influenced by their nomadism.

Since they must travel with as few possessions as possible, they own only the necessary minimum. They also adapt their clothing to their environment, generally dressing the way the peasants do in whatever country they are living or passing through. Gypsies in Spain will wear the same kind of clothing that the Spanish wear, and the Gypsies in Hungary are hardly distinguishable, as far as dress is concerned, from the Hungarian peasants.

Nonetheless, the stereotype of the Gypsy woman with the long, colorful skirt, the heavy earrings, and often a flower in her hair has some basis in fact. Traditionally, a woman's legs must not show. Exposure of the legs is a grave offense, so long, full skirts must be worn. The reasons for this are uncertain, but it is probable that long skirts were once thought of as protection against sexual advances. They also cover the lower part of the body, which is considered "impure." These skirts are generally of very bright colors, sometimes made of worn bits and pieces sewn together, often consisting of many layers. Except for color, a Gypsy woman does not have a varied wardrobe.

Jewelry is a different matter, and Gypsy women are very fond of earrings, bracelets, necklaces of beads or silver or gold, and elaborate, heavy buttons. They treasure jewelry not only for its beauty, but for its intrinsic value. They do not have bank accounts or safe-deposit boxes, so they feel most secure carrying their valuables on their own bodies.

As for men, there is really no characteristic clothing. For festive occasions, they will wear a good suit and show a preference for bright colors; most of them own one suit at a time and wear it until it is threadbare. Generally, however, their clothing is indistinguishable from that of the people they live or travel among.

Traditionally, too, the eating habits of Gypsies have been conditioned by their nomadic way of life. They have not been fishermen, farmers, or hunters, so their diet has consisted largely of what was readily available. This included wild fruits, berries, molluscs, rodents, and snakes. These wanderers were also known to eat the carcasses of dead animals—cattle or sheep or hogs who had died of disease and were left by the roadside. Before cooking, they were generally buried in the ground for twenty-four hours so that they might become tenderized. While non-Gypsies are horrified at the idea of eating such meat, the Gypsies reason that animal diseases cannot infect human beings, and moreover, that "the best meat is that given to us by God"—in other words, the meat of animals who have died a natural death and have not been slaughtered by man.

As the Gypsies have gradually come into greater contact with people of the cities, their eating habits have conformed more and more to those of the non-Gypsy. A Gypsy's day will generally begin with very strong black coffee, heavily sweetened with sugar. Coffee is a staple of Gypsy existence, and many cups are taken in the course of a day.

There is usually no lunch, and dinner is served at sunset, or, since the food is generally on the stove all afternoon, whenever anyone is hungry. It is prepared by a daughter-in-law, the mother, or the eldest daughter living with her family. The basic element of this dinner is a thick, fatty vegetable soup or stew—any available vegetables or greens are put into it, and it is usually made even more hearty by the addition of potatoes, rice, or pasta. Sometimes meat is served, generally broiled or cooked on a spit. Game and fowl, too, are enjoyed when possible. Garlic is the most heavily used of all seasonings.

Bread is seldom eaten. Gypsy women do not bake it, and, in fact, it is more often carried as a protection against evil spirits than used as a food. Instead of bread, however, maize cakes are served. As far as beverages are concerned, water is most often served during the course of a meal.

Festive occasions are, of course, different, and during such celebrations the Gypsies uninhibitedly indulge their hearty appetites. Gypsy living is most often austere and hard; the only times to be extravagant are special occasions.

At such times, enormous quantities of food and drink are consumed, and the preparation is long and enthusiastic. A favorite dish has traditionally been roast hedgehog, a rich and succulent meat with a pork-like flavor, which is also enjoyed by some non-Gypsy Europeans. Ideally, this animal, skin and all, and flavored with garlic, is wrapped in clay and then placed on burning hot stones. In this way, it cooks in its own fat. When the roasting is completed, the clay is removed—and attached to it are the animals' prickles. The meat is then wrapped in aromatic leaves and served. Chicken and other fowl can also be cooked this way.

On these special days, alcohol—beer, whiskey, and occasionally wine—is substituted for water at the meal, and it is not unusual for far more than normal quantities of alcohol to be consumed. This happens only on these days, and heavy drinking is otherwise uncommon among the

Gypsies. A misconception, with no basis in fact, is that Gypsies are often drunk.

Another misconception is that they will eat anything they can get their hands on. While undoubtedly true that their wandering existence and poverty have forced them to eat foods that might be distasteful to other peoples, there are very strict taboos against certain foods, chief among them horsemeat, which is eaten by non-Gypsies in many parts of the world. Any Gypsy eating horsemeat will be severely punished or even banished from the tribe; the relationship of the horse to the Gypsy has always been such a close one that it is unthinkable to eat this animal. Cats and dogs are also forbidden as foods. These animals have no special meaning for the Gypsies, but they consider them unclean because they lick themselves.

Cleanliness is a very special matter for the Gypsy, one that is little understood by outsiders, who most often consider Gypsies a dirty people, unconcerned about personal hygiene. This misunderstanding is certainly encouraged by the Gypsy who often wants to appear dirty, knowing that this is one sure way of avoiding close contact with the Gaje—whom he or she really thinks of as dirty.

The Gypsy code of hygiene is based on the concept of *marime*—it is a complex and rigid system. An understanding of this fundamental part of Gypsy life will make it clear why the Gypsies feel that the Gaje are unclean.

This *marime* is related to the *marime* concept adopted by the Gypsy courts, but while the legal term means "rejected," the term when applied to personal hygiene means "dirty" or "polluted." Much of it stems from the division of a Gypsy woman's body into two parts—above the waist and below the waist. A woman is clean from the waist up and "polluted" from the waist down. There is no shame connected with the upper part of the body; women are allowed to expose their breasts, and they will often use their brassieres as pocketbooks. There is nothing wrong with a man reaching into a woman's brassiere to take a few coins.

The lower part of the body is, however, an object of shame because it is associated with menstruation. The belief that menstruation is a sign of impurity is not unique among Gypsies and is widespread among many primitive societies. The fact that blood flows without injury seems to be, for these societies, the proof of a bodily impurity, located in the lower part of a woman's body.

Many of the traditional laws of hygiene deal with water. For example, a Gypsy must wash only in running water. A shower would be acceptable, but a bath would not be, for the Gypsy would be sitting or lying in dirty, stagnant water. Dishes cannot be rinsed in the same sink or basin that is used for washing personal clothing. The kitchen sink is used only for washing dishes, and therefore it cannot ever be used for washing one's hands. In addition, women's clothes and men's clothes cannot be washed together, because of the impurities of the women's bodies.

Certain Gypsy tribes have set specific and very rigid rules for the drawing of water from a river or stream. The water from the farthest point upstream, therefore the purest, is used for drinking and cooking. Working their way downstream, the water is used in this order: washing dishes and bathing; washing or nourishing horses; washing clothes; and, at the nearest point downstream, washing the clothes of pregnant or menstruating women. In order to make certain that there will be no impurities,

Gypsies have special rules for washing dishes.

separate pails are always used for the different uses of water.

Some traditional rules might make sense to a non-Gypsy. The surfaces of tables used for eating are kept spotless; shoes or underwear must never be placed on an eating surface. Handkerchiefs are frowned upon—they merely preserve the dirt of the nose, and for this reason Gypsies prefer to blow their noses in material such as paper that can be thrown away. In any case, after blowing his or her nose or sneezing, a Gypsy must wash before eating.

Indoor toilets used by many people are thought of as unsanitary, and whenever possible a Gypsy will use a hedge. The very idea of keeping a separate room as a toilet is repugnant to many Gypsies—this calls attention to what, for the Gypsy, is an unclean act. However, when an indoor toilet is used—and nowadays this is generally the case—a guard is often posted at the door to make certain that no member of the opposite sex enters the room by mistake.

The concept of *marime* as applied to women is one explanation for the use of long skirts and the fact that the bottom of those skirts must not touch a man other than the Gypsy woman's husband—or else that man, even by unintentional contact, will become infected. Even if a woman's skirt inadvertently brushes up against plates, cups, or glasses, those objects become *marime* and then might soil the next man who eats or drinks from them. They must therefore be destroyed.

There are other rules. A woman in a house must not pass in front of a man, or even between two men; she must go around them in order to avoid infecting them. At meals, the men must be served from the rear for the same reason. And if a Gypsy woman is not wearing the traditional long skirt, she must cover her legs with a blanket or coat when sitting.

Any object that becomes *marime* must be destroyed; dishes are broken and clothing is burned. If not, these objects are infected with evil, and that evil is highly contagious.

There are, of course, other remedies or punishments for a person who is infected in such a way. Minor offenses, clearly unintentional ones, can be forgiven by those present at the time the offense is committed, but more serious ones must be dealt with by the community and, in some cases, by the *kris*.

VII

Birth

FROM THE MOMENT OF BIRTH, THE GYPSY IS SUBJECT TO the laws and customs developed over centuries and embodied by the *kris*. While the severity of many traditional laws has lessened with time, traces of them still remain, though they vary from tribe to tribe and from country to country. Gypsy life has been a life of hardship, of constant exposure to cold winters and hot summers, of an endless wandering from place to place. For these reasons, severity has been essential for survival, and special rites are observed at the times of birth, marriage, and death.

Strict rules come into effect before the actual birth of the child—at the time of pregnancy. Most of these rules are based on the belief that a woman is *marime*, impure, during pregnancy and for a period of time after the birth of the infant. As soon as a woman is certain that she is preg-

62

nant, she tells her husband and other women of the community. It is a proud moment, and the pregnancy signals a decided change in her status among the group. The prospect of a newborn child is a cause for much joy; Gypsies take great pride in having large families to carry on their traditions. However, pregnancy also means that the woman is impure and must be isolated as much as possible from the community. She is cared for only by other women in the community, and her husband can spend only short periods of time with her during the pregnancy, though she continues to live at home. It is frequently his job, too, to take over the domestic duties when she is unable to handle them.

The birth itself cannot take place in the family's usual home, whether it be a tent or a trailer, because it would then become impure and have to be destroyed. Because of this, women have given birth in fields, in haylofts, or in tents specially built for use during delivery (and then destroyed). In spite of their contempt for non-Gypsy ways, an increasing number of Gypsy women have preferred to leave their encampments and give birth in a hospital—not because they think they will receive better care, but because in that way they will not soil their own homes. If the delivery of the infant is to take place outside a hospital, only specially appointed midwives, or possibly other women who have experienced maternity, are allowed to assist.

There are any number of magic rites that might precede the actual birth, the most common of which involves the untying of certain knots—so that the umbilical cord will not be knotted. Sometimes all the knots in clothing will be undone or cut; other times, the mother-to-be's hair will be loosened if it has been pinned or tied with a ribbon.

Several rituals, too, have traditionally followed the birth of the infant. A most frequently practiced one is the purification of the child, washing it in running water, an act that is separate from any subsequent baptism. After washing, the child might be massaged with oil in order to

The crib of a Gypsy baby consists of a blanket fastened to a carriage beam.

strengthen it; in some cases, amulets or talismans are used to protect it from evil spirits.

Other symbolic rituals involve the formal recognition of the infant by its father. In some cases, the child is wrapped in swaddling on which a few drops of paternal blood are placed. In other cases, the child is covered by a piece of clothing that belongs to the father, and in some tribes it is traditional for the mother to put the infant on the ground, from which it is picked up by the father, who places a red string around its neck, thereby acknowledging that the child is his.

Childbirth itself does not end the state of the mother's impurity, it continues until the time of the infant's baptism. This baptism takes place any time from a few weeks to a few months after birth—most commonly between two and three weeks. During this interim period, the mother and child are both isolated from the community.

The mother cannot be seen by any man except, in some tribes, by the husband. The husband, too, faces restrictions, since he will often be forbidden from going out between sunset and sunrise to keep away evil spirits, which might attack the infant during the night. These evil spirits might attack the new mother, too, but only other women—and never her husband or other men—are allowed to protect her, because of her impure condition.

A new mother is allowed to touch only essential objects—and in some cases not even those—during what amounts to a period of quarantine. The objects she does touch, such as cooking and eating utensils or sheets, become impure and must be destroyed.

Though all this generally ends with the baby's baptism, certain groups are unusually cautious. For these groups, it is two or three months before the new mother will be able to approach her husband or perform household duties without the use of gloves.

The newborn child is also considered impure until he or she is baptized. Before that, its name cannot be pronounced, it cannot be photographed, and sometimes the baby's face is not even permitted to be shown in public. This period does not end until the baptism, when the impurities are washed away by immersion in running water. After that purification, the infant formally becomes a human being and can then be called by a name. This name, however, is only one of three that the child will carry through his or her life.

The first name given remains forever a secret; it is generally whispered by the mother, the only one who knows it, at the time of birth and is never used. The purpose of this secret name is to confuse the demons by keeping the real identity of the child from them. The second name is a Gypsy name, the one used only among the Gypsies themselves. It is conferred informally and only among Gypsies. Prevalent among Gypsies are colorful names such as Pulika, Terkari, Chavula, and Bidshika for boys, and Tekla, Saviya, Tshaya, and Rupa for girls. The third name is given at a second baptism which takes place according to the customs of the dominant religion of the country in which the child happens to be born. It has little importance for the Gypsies and is merely a practical necessity, to be used for dealing with non-Gypsies.

VIII

Marriage

THE CHILDHOOD OF A GYPSY IS AN UNDISCIPLINED ONE; indeed, in certain ways Gypsy parents might be called unusually permissive according to non-Gypsy standards. That is not to say that the years of growing up are easy ones; obviously, the rigors and difficulties of the Gypsies' nomadic existence serve to toughen the child.

However, there is little discipline as such. The growing child plays at will, improvising entertainments without the aid of special games or toys. There is no organized entertainment. He or she learns whatever skills can be acquired from the mother or father, first by imitating them, and, finally, by helping out his parents whenever possible. He or she learns the ways of the Gypsies, too, by observation and, at a certain point, participation.

Participation, however, is not complete until the time of

A Gypsy child amuses his family and friends.

marriage. Engagements and marriages are the greatest events, the most joyous times in the life of a Gypsy; they are the most happily and uninhibitedly celebrated of all periods. Bachelorhood is held in contempt as an unnatural condition, while marriage is an essential, basic fact of life. Until he is married (and most Gypsies marry while in their teens), even if he is fifty years old, a male Gypsy cannot be called a *Rom*.

There are few rules regarding marriage, except that a Gypsy is discouraged, if not forbidden, from marrying a non-Gypsy. He or she is also expected to marry someone within the particular tribe. This is a way of maintaining racial purity and individuality. There are exceptional cases, in which a Gypsy might take a non-Gypsy bride, but the latter is expected to renounce her former ways and take up completely and faithfully the Gypsy way of life. However, this is a rarity, and most Gypsies conform by marrying within their group.

The first step in contemplating marriage is the selection of the bride, and this all-important move varies from group to group. In many parts of the world, this is done just as it would be done in non-Gypsy society. The boy does the courting, and when the young couple agree to marry they become engaged and exchange modest gifts. Parents are consulted, but the decision is made by the young people.

In many other parts of the world, however, it is the parents—and not the young people—who arrange the marriage. The prospective bride and groom might be consulted, but they don't really count. According to these groups, it is an essential and important duty of the parents to find a bride suitable for their son. They carefully consider all the young, unmarried women in the group, evaluating their individual qualities. Looks are of the least importance, and the prospective brides are judged on their health, stamina, strength; on their dispositions, manners, their attitudes toward children, and their skills—if they can cook, if they are adept at telling fortunes, if they can maintain a proper home. The character of the girl's family, as well as its prestige in the community, is also taken into account.

In these cases, no courtship is involved, and it is possible that the prospective couple will hardly know each other, though there most probably would have been some contact in the encampment. They will usually send a third, uninvolved person to sound out the girl's parents on the acceptability of the young man. Rejection of a formal proposal is considered a disgrace and is not to be risked. If all goes well, the father of the boy then calls on the father of the girl. It is a polite and rather serious meeting, the purpose being not only to obtain the formal consent of the girl's father, but to establish a price to be paid for the bride. This money to be exchanged should be thought of not as purchase of a bride, but rather in terms of compensation to the father for the loss of his daughter.

The discussion can be a long one, centering on the estimated value of the future bride. All the would-be bride's desired qualities are taken into consideration; in addition, the girl's father calculates how much his daughter has cost him since birth. After all, since she will live and work with her husband's family, he is in effect giving her away, and his money and training have helped make her what she is.

At these meetings, there might well be violent disagreements. Sometimes it is necessary to call in friends as witnesses to the bride's good qualities, to argue for a higher price on her behalf; or to call in other friends to arbitrate.

When an agreement is reached, and the price is accepted, the meeting ends with the father of the bride-to-be drinking a symbolic glass of wine. This means that the boy has been formally approved as a husband for his daughter, under the stipulated conditions.

Before the wedding.

The men gather before the wedding.

This arrangement has, throughout the years, become
somewhat less common. Because of greater knowledge of
non-Gypsy societies, many young couples have rebelled
against these arranged marriages and against any kind of
engagement and have eloped. Elopement consists simply
of leaving the camp together for a period of time. When
they return they are chastised—some must pay a nominal
fine—but eventually they are accepted as a married
couple.

Most young Gypsies, however, do not elope, and for

them there is a long period of lively celebration. Following the formal agreement of terms, there is often a huge banquet, complete with singing and dancing. The bride-to-be and her family often feign great, exaggerated sorrow at having to leave each other. The groom's family, on the other hand, pretend to be angry that they are paying such a high price for the bride. In the end, they decide that the price is well worth it for a bride who will clearly be such a good wife to their son.

Frequently, a few days after the agreement has been made, a ceremony called a *plotchka* (or *pliashka*) will be held. This event is attended by both friends and relatives of the couple.

The symbol of this joyous celebration is a bottle of wine or brandy wrapped in a brightly colored silk handkerchief, brought to the ceremony by the young man's father. A necklace of gold coins is attached to the bottle. When the groom-to-be and his father arrive, the father pretends to look for something he has lost. He anxiously circles the room; finally, he spots the girl and points a finger at her. He then takes the necklace of coins, puts it around her neck, and warmly embraces his future daughter-in-law. The necklace makes it clear to all that the girl is now engaged and not available as a bride to any other man. Her father-in-law-to-be drinks from the bottle and passes it around to the guests. When the bottle is emptied, it is refilled for use at the wedding celebration.

The wedding itself is largely a symbolic act, with no religious significance. Though Gypsies usually have had to conform to local laws and customs in the countries in which they marry, the non-Gypsy religious or civil ceremonies have little or no meaning for them. The mere fact

The bride leaves for the ceremony.

that two people have agreed to live together and share their lives together constitutes marriage, and no formal ritual is required. This does not mean that they don't take marriage seriously, but rather that they do not believe in the importance of a formal wedding ceremony under the jurisdiction of a church or a state.

Nonetheless, there are traditional but simple wedding ceremonies performed by some groups of Gypsies. In some marriages, the bride and groom will join hands in front of the chief of a tribe, or an elder of that tribe, and promise to be true to each other. A colorful ceremony, once followed, was called "Jumping the Broomstick." This meant that the couple were considered married after having jumped over a broom in the presence of their families or other witnesses.

A few Gypsy wedding rites are centered around bread. In one, the bride and groom each take a piece of bread and place a drop of their blood on the bread. They then exchange and eat each other's bread. In another ritual, the young couple sit down, surrounded by relatives and friends. A small amount of salt and bread is then placed on the knees of the bride. The groom takes some of the bread, puts salt on it, and eats it; the bride does the same. The surrounding well-wishers then toast the couple, asking that they might live together in harmony as do salt and bread.

The informal, joyous festivities celebrating the marriage can go on for several days, until the guests are weary. No expense is spared, and fortunes—borrowed, stolen, or saved—are spent on these happy occasions. Excess is the rule, and moderation the exception, as the Gypsies enjoy themselves with an abandon they can seldom afford.

A huge feast is served, and that in itself is an extraordinary event in the life of these people who generally live so frugally. There is usually an open fire over which whole pigs, sides of beef, game, chicken, or goose are roasted. If it is available, hedgehog will be served. There might be huge platters of fried potatoes and boiled cabbage stuffed with rice and chopped meat and flavored with herbs and garlic. Drink, too, is served as generously as is food: wine, whiskey, and beer flow endlessly for this banquet. Violinists play happy, rhythmic tunes; there are songs and dances. The atmosphere is a festive one; the Gypsies are dressed in their finest clothes, and they enjoy themselves as they rarely do.

When the celebration ends, and the crowd is ready to leave the gaily colored tent where the festivities have been held, it is time for the groom to take his bride to his home. The bride's family kisses the girl and they weep as they unbraid her hair, a symbol for her new marital status.

Before the groom can take her home, however, there might be an amusing game of the feigned abduction of the bride, whose unmarried friends link arms and form a wall in front of the girl in order to protect her from him. The friends of the groom try, for their part, to break the wall so that the groom might abduct his bride. There is much playacting, a great deal of screaming and crying on the part of the bride's protectors, but the groom, happily, always wins, proudly leading his new bride to his family home, which will be their home.

The following morning, it is very important that there be some sort of proof of the bride's virginity—either a blood-stained handkerchief or a blood-stained sheet is displayed as evidence. In some cases, however, an examination by some of the older women of the tribe is conducted for this purpose before the wedding.

Whatever the proof, when it has been established, her new mother-in-law helps the bride knot her kerchief, a sign that she is a married woman. She is never again without this kerchief in public.

The celebrations ended, a new life begins for the couple, who now take their places as full members of the community. The major change for the man is that he is now socially accepted by other married men, and his social life revolves around them and not around his bachelor friends. Changes for the woman are more radical, for it is she who leaves her family, gathers her eiderdown quilt and her personal belongings, and moves in with her husband's family. She is guided by her new mother-in-law and expected to take an active role in the household. Not until the birth of their first child—or sometimes not until the birth of several children—will the couple move into their own tent or trailer. Not until they are parents, too, will they be able to refer to each other as husband and wife; before that, they use only their first names with each other or in speaking about each other.

Marriages among Gypsies are serious commitments, and there are strict obligations on both sides. If a girl is found guilty of adultery, she must be taken back by her parents, who, in addition, must return the bridal price to the husband's father; or, if the girl's father feels she has been mistreated by her husband or her in-laws, he has the right to take her away. In many cases, these complaints are heard before the *kris* before a final settlement is made.

IX

Death

BIRTH, MARRIAGE, AND—FINALLY—DEATH: THE THREE
most significant occasions for the Gypsies, as they are for
most people. Just as with birth and marriage, these people
have their own rites and traditions, which are associated
with the advent of death, the burial of the deceased, and
the post-funeral mourning period.

Death for the Gypsies is the worst of fates; it is a sense-
less unnatural occurrence which should, justifiably, anger
those who die. Because of this, at the approach of death,
the Gypsy is concerned not only with the pain and
heartbreak of the final separation from a loved one, but he
or she is also profoundly worried about the possible revenge the angry dead might seek against those who remain in the world of the living.

78

Death

There are many superstitious portents of death, the most common of which is the cry of the owl. This crying of the owl, however, means approaching death in many societies and is not unique among the Gypsies. Obviously, a more certain sign of death is serious illness, and when the Gypsies feel that one of their group is about to die, word is urgently sent to all relatives, no matter how far away they might be.

As we have learned, through fixed contact points—the *vurma*—Gypsies are able to find one another in time of need, even without fixed addresses. When an emergency, such as approaching death, arises, relatives and friends can be reached, and especially in the case of death, all relatives who can possibly do so appear at the bedside of the man or woman who is reaching the end of his life. It is necessary to show family solidarity, and to obtain forgiveness for any evil act they might have committed toward the dying in the past. There must be no danger of a lingering hidden envy or secret resentment on the part of those who are about to begin a journey to the world of the dead.

The dying Gypsy must never be left alone—not only out of compassion for his condition, but also for fear of possible anger. He or she must not die in his or her habitual place, and because of this a bed is normally moved in front of the tent or caravan, usually under an improvised wall-less canopy. Relatives and friends gather around the dying Gypsy, day and night, while other Gypsies in the camp take care of practical matters such as feeding the visitors and tracking down those friends or relatives who have been difficult to reach. There are not only tears and lamentations, but rage is expressed at the horrors of approaching death.

Touching the body of the deceased is discouraged, for fear of contamination. Because of this he or she is washed and dressed—in the finest clothes—immediately preceding death. If death has been unexpected and this has not been possible, a non-Gypsy is usually called in to perform these tasks immediately following the death.

When death finally comes, the wailing and moaning increase, and from that time until the burial, certain traditional customs are observed. Above all, there is total absorption in the mourning, with no everyday distractions or activities. There is no washing or shaving or combing of the hair. No food is prepared. Only the drinking of coffee, brandy, or other liquors is permitted. Mirrors might be covered and vessels containing water emptied.

An important step, too, is the gathering together of those things that will be useful to the deceased during the journey from life, objects that will be placed in the coffin. These can include almost anything—clothing, tools, eating utensils, a watch, a pipe, a violin, things of value such as favored silver or gold ornaments, and almost always a small amount of money.

The funeral itself, though of little or no religious significance, is impressive and moving. Often a band, made up of non-Gypsies, goes ahead of the coffin, playing marches. This band is followed by the widow or widower, other mourning relatives and, if local religious customs must be followed, by a priest. As this procession enters the cemetery, the sobbing of the mourners borders on hysteria. The women might pull their hair, or tear their clothes; their grief is unrestrained.

This display of rage and sorrow reaches its peak as the coffin is lowered into the grave. Sometimes the widow will even try to throw herself on top of the coffin. The mourners generally throw silver and gold coins and bank notes as well as handfuls of earth into the grave.

The color worn by mourners at Gypsy funerals—until recent times, when the non-Gypsy's black is sometimes adopted—has traditionally been white or red. White has been thought of as a symbol of purity, of protection, and of good luck. Many Gypsy women will dress entirely in white, and the men will wear white ties and gloves and place white bands around their hats.

Red, too, has symbolized protection against the evil spirits of the dead and has often been worn at Gypsy funerals. Gypsies feel that the color red brings good luck and are probably drawn to it because of the ancient belief that blood is the source of vitality and life. Red blouses and skirts are common apparel for women at funerals, and men often wear red kerchiefs around their necks. Red, too, is a predominant color in many Gypsy funeral decorations.

There is inevitably a large crowd at a Gypsy funeral. It is an occasion for friends and family to unite, to wish the departed a good journey as he or she enters a new life. We often read colorful newspaper accounts of the elaborate funerals presumably held for an "important" Gypsy, but it must be remembered that a huge funeral is the rule and not the exception in Gypsy society, and all Gypsies are entitled to enormous funerals.

Following the burial, the dead man or woman will, of course, be remembered for the acts he or she performed on earth, but all material ties with the dead must be carefully destroyed. Whatever can be burned, such as clothing and linens, will be turned into ashes; articles such as

Mourners returning from a funeral.

plates, cups, glasses, or jewelry that belonged to the dead will be broken or mutilated. Even animals that belonged to the dead must be killed. Only the horse is usually excluded from this rule.

Since this obviously imposes great financial hardship on the surviving family, it has become more and more usual to sell these objects rather than destroy them, but they are sold only to non-Gypsies. No Gypsy would consider risking contamination by accepting or buying them. There should be no trace of the deceased in the Gypsy camp—even the use of his or her name is avoided, except when absolutely necessary.

Another tradition which follows the funeral is a dinner called a *Pomana*. It is an enormous meal, usually the first one eaten by the mourners since the death of their friend or relative. Sometimes even the deceased is represented at these meals, by another person of the same age as the deceased and dressed in a similar way. These *Pomana* are held at various intervals—usually nine days, six weeks, six months, and, finally, one year after the death. At each of these *Pomana*, certain relatives, beginning with the most distant ones, announce their intention to end their period of mourning. Last to do so, after one year, are the deceased's immediate family.

There is no heaven and hell, according to the Gypsies; life for the dead continues on another level. However, there is a great fear among the survivors that the dead might return in some form to haunt the living. It is for this reason that the name of the dead should not be mentioned, that the body should not be touched, and that all objects that belonged to the dead must be destroyed. The survivors must be protected in every way from the evil, contaminating spirits that the dead can emit. To avoid this, stones or thorn bushes are sometimes placed around the grave.

According to the Gypsies, the soul of the dead might be reincarnated in another man or animal, but most feared of all is the possible reappearance of the dead in the form of a *mulo* or vampire. Unless strict precautions are taken, this *mulo*—which means "living dead"—might escape from the body and seek revenge on those who had harmed him when living or had caused his death. The mere sight of a *mulo,* who can appear as a vampire or a wolf, terrorizes the Gypsy; it is a certain sign of bad luck.

Superstition obviously plays a significant role in many aspects of Gypsy life. However, of all their rites, those connected with death are more filled with fear and super-stition than any others.

X

Gypsies Today

WHATEVER METHODS THEY HAVE USED IN THE PAST, NON-Gypsies have been unable to eliminate the presence of these alien people, since Gypsies today are found in almost every part of the world—Europe, North Africa, South Africa, Australia, South America, and the United States. They still constitute a social problem wherever they go, and our modern "enlightened" societies have, for the most part, dealt with this problem by attempting to assimilate these people, encouraging or forcing them to abandon their traditional ways of life and adapt to non-Gypsy ways. The results of these attempts have varied from country to country, according to local conditions.

The largest number of Gypsies are still to be found in Europe, even after the exterminations of World War II. France, which had eleven concentration camps just for

86

The Gypsies Today

Gypsies during the war, is estimated to be the home of approximately one hundred thousand Gypsies, three quarters of whom have settled in or on the fringes of cities. Most live in crowded segregated quarters. They are discriminated against by city dwellers and feared by peasants, who automatically close their windows and lock their doors at the approach of a Gypsy. Some attempts have been made to educate the Gypsies and make them French, but these attempts have met with little success. Camping sites are few, and throughout the country many

A Gypsy camp outside Paris.

French police check passports.

signs are posted saying "Gypsies forbidden." At best, the Gypsies constitute a tourist attraction at their annual pilgrimage each May in the Camargue. The status of the Gypsies as second-class citizens was confirmed by an extraordinary 1912 law. According to this law, all nomadic Gypsies must report regularly to the local police and must carry special identity cards that include such absurd information as the length of finger, the size of the right ear and the left foot, and the exact distance from the middle finger to the elbow.

In Italy, too, conditions for the Gypsy are unfavorable. There have been halfhearted attempts to integrate them into Italian society and to set up permanent housing for them, but for the most part the Gypsies living on the outskirts of large cities are feared and mistrusted by the native population and harassed by the police.

Modern Gypsies have fared better in less industrialized countries, where their way of life and traditional occupations blend in more easily with the native rural communities. Spain is one example of a country in which the Gypsies have apparently integrated with considerable success. Many have settled in Spanish cities and have attained equal social status with the Spaniards.

Above all, Spanish Gypsies have been appreciated as entertainers. Their contributions to the music and dance of the country continue to be acknowledged. One particularly interesting Gypsy group, which can number as many as three thousand at a time, lives in caves found in Sacro Monte, a hill dominating the city of Granada. Living conditions there are good—the caves are cool in summer and warm in winter—and these Gypsies make a comfortable living by performing for and selling their handicrafts to

A Hungarian Gypsy village.

the tourists. They are effectively able to maintain their traditional ways of life within the country's social structure.

Hungary, too, where more than 150,000 Gypsies are found, is proud of its Gypsy performers. Bands perform throughout the country, and Gypsy musicians are respected and admired. Nomadism, however, has been outlawed since the end of World War II, and Gypsies who refused to settle were forced to leave the country. Those who remained have generally adapted: horse trading has been forbidden and has been replaced by coal mining; artisan toolmakers have turned their skills to the manufacture of building materials.

Other eastern European countries have made serious and well-intentioned efforts to assimilate their Gypsy populations, without, however, allowing the Gypsies to live as nomads. The government of Czechoslovakia has helped these people find jobs and homes and has even set up special open-air schools where handicrafts and violin-playing are taught. The Gypsies have in this way been encouraged to carry on their traditional occupations, yet their basic way of life—nomadism—was officially banned in 1958. A plan to achieve total social assimilation by 1980 has been in effect; since more than half the Gypsy population in Czechoslovakia is under eighteen years old, and thus more easily adaptable, hopes have been high for this "benign" elimination of the Gypsies.

Nonetheless, there have been difficulties in Czechoslovakia—as there have been in Yugoslavia—where the state has provided modern apartments in housing projects for the Gypsies. The Gypsies have dutifully moved into these new homes, filled them with their possessions, and then quickly moved out—camping in front of these modern buildings.

The Soviet Union, too, has made a serious effort to assimilate its Gypsy population, but it, too, has encountered problems. Nomadism was outlawed in 1956, and the government embarked on an ambitious program to help settle these wandering people while allowing them to retain their separate cultural identity. Homes were found for them, and they were trained to work on collective farms and take their places in workers' cooperatives. At the same time, special schools were established, a Romany-language newspaper was founded, and Gypsy literature and theater were encouraged.

This elaborate program seemed to be working well, and the government was proud of its achievement. However, after a few years, there were signs that the Gypsies had found it impossible to conform to Soviet ways. A law was passed stating that Gypsies not performing socially useful work could be sent to work camps for up to five years—this meant that there were a considerable number of Gypsies who were not doing such work. From that time on, far less has been heard about Soviet achievements in integrating the Gypsies into a new way of life, and there have been indications that no serious efforts are being made to enforce the laws banning nomadism.

Great Britain, too, has had problems with its fifteen thousand Gypsies, most of whom live in rural areas of England and Wales. Life for them was relatively simple—they worked as artisans, smiths, and horse traders—until 1936, when the first of a series of laws was passed that effectively outlawed their way of life. "Acts of God they allowed for," wrote Alastair Reid, "but Acts of Parliament they neither knew of nor could foresee until suddenly they found themselves tumbled off the tiny plateau on which they had been quite happy to live."

These many laws have varied throughout the years, but all of them have placed restrictions on the nomadic existence of these people whom William Wordsworth called the "wild outcasts of society." There have been laws against overcrowding in tents or trailers—a condition natural to the Gypsy. They have been forbidden to camp on land, even their own, if it is against "interests of proper planning of their area." They have not been allowed to encamp near a highway, a logical place for them to rest, and they have been unable to park their trailers in any site without a license, even with the owner's permission.

In 1968, the British Parliament passed the Caravan Sites Act, a law that required local authorities to provide trailer parks for Gypsies and other itinerants. This bill, presumably in favor of the Gypsies, actually restricted them to stopping only in legally designated areas, no matter what their needs might be. Stopping elsewhere meant a heavy fine. The second part of the same act was passed in 1970, further preventing the Gypsies from pursuing their normal activities. Among its provisions was a limitation on the number of pets allowed and the ban of all open fires —an integral part of the Gypsy way of life.

The Gypsies' lot in Great Britain—in spite of the concern of many journalists, members of Parliament, and the active Gypsy Lore Society, the major source of information concerning the Gypsies and their traditions—has remained a difficult one. They are barred from using sites that have served them for generations, either by law or by the construction of large housing projects. The sites provided for them are too few, and most have inadequate washing and toilet facilities and no garbage collection. The Gypsies are constantly subject to harassment by the police, and there is always one law or another that can be applied against them.

Because of the frustrations that result from these restrictive laws, many Gypsies have moved into homes or apartments. However, the majority of them are unhappy there. They feel that they are contaminated by the world of the non-Gypsy—by the factory smoke, the polluted air, and the poisoned rivers. They yearn to return to the open road, their true home. What they ask for are permanent camps for the old, a large number of conveniently located sites for short stops, and adequately equipped and reasonably priced campsites where they might spend the cold winters. They ask, too, for education so that they might cope with the law and understand and make use of Britain's social welfare system and its benefits.

Because of the vastness of the country and the fact that it is composed of so many foreign minorities, the Gypsies are less visible in the United States than elsewhere. Most Americans are totally unaware of their presence, and, according to census and immigration figures, they do not even exist. Nonetheless, large numbers of Gypsies began arriving in the latter part of the nineteenth century— mostly from eastern Europe and Spain (via South America)—and according to most estimates there are approximately two hundred thousand Gypsies in the United States today. Their problems are somewhat different than they have been in Europe, and in some ways the Gypsies have suffered less directly than their European counterparts because they are less noticed by the American people.

Generally, the Gypsies of America have had to give up a full-time nomadic existence. As in other countries, horses were, of course, replaced by motor vehicles—cars, large buses, trailers, and campers—and these require large quantities of gas, which has proved too costly for most Gypsies. Free camping sites, too, are scarce. For these reasons, most Gypsies, while retaining their mobili-

A fortune-teller.

ty and keeping open all possibilities for travel, have temporarily settled in the poor areas of major cities, renting small ground-floor apartments whenever possible.

The men generally work on short-term jobs that don't require them to stay in one place for any length of time; they have been able to find such jobs since they will accept work that non-Gypsies will shun. Their love for horses has been transferred to a love for cars, and they are often skilled body repairmen or auto mechanics. But they insist on maintaining their independence by refusing work that will tie them to non-Gypsy employers, never, for example, taking steady work in a garage, but undertaking one job at a time such as the repair of a single car.

It is the Gypsy women who, in the United States as elsewhere, earn most of the money. The easiest and most "honorable" way of doing this is through fortune-telling. As soon as possible after their arrival in a city, fortune-tellers rent a storefront, with a room or two in the back. These are usually located in poor business areas of the city, though some Gypsies are now setting up practices in some of the more fashionable streets of cities like New York.

The back area is for living, and it is still likely to look like a traditional Gypsy camp with little furniture, and with draperies and rags and rugs hung or strewn about the room, a mattress or two on the floor, and some kind of portable stove or hot plate for cooking.

The storefront itself is set up as an *ofisa*—the place of business. It is from there that the Gypsies solicit their clients and perform their work. Some of these *ofisas* are dark and dingy; others are astoundingly luxurious. All contain an aura of mystery.

97

The most frequent visitors to Gypsy fortune-tellers are middle-aged women who are troubled and depressed, often under tension, and usually suffering from problems with which they are unable to cope. They turn to fortune-tellers not only for soothing predictions, but for concrete advice, and often they feel that these Gypsy women are the only ones who will listen to their sad stories.

If a fortune-teller believes that the client is merely curious, one fortune-telling session, at whatever price can be extracted, will suffice. Depending on the client's gullibility and emotional condition, the Gypsy might decide that further sessions are called for—at increasingly higher prices. If the client is unusually desperate and troubled, the ultimate and most profitable of Gypsy confidence games will be attempted—the Bajour or Boojoo. This word means "bag," or "bag of money," and the bag itself is an essential part of this elaborate swindle. Once the fortune-teller has learned that her gullible client has money—either in a savings bank or hidden in her home—she announces that the client's troubles are due to a curse on that money. This curse can only be removed by the Gypsy's supernatural powers. The money is then dutifully brought to the Gypsy, who places it in a bag that is carefully tied—and, most important, substituted by a bag containing worthless scraps of paper. The substituted bag is then blessed by the Gypsy, who is likely to perform an elaborate ceremony for the occasion. The removal of the curse has begun, and the mystified client is told to take the bag home and wait for a period of time—at least twenty-four hours—before opening it and removing the newly purified money.

As instructed, the client later opens the bag, only to find

Sign in a window in Washington, D.C.

not money but worthless pieces of paper. More humiliated than angry, she will usually return to the *ofisa*. Inevitably, it is too late; the Gypsy has moved on and is never found. Most victimized women are too embarrassed to go to the police, or even to tell their relatives or friends of the hoax, and so few Gypsies are caught.

In addition to their talents as fortune-tellers, Gypsy women have used their intuitive skills in dealing with social workers and welfare officers. They are experts in "beating the system," in exaggerating their poverty and their needs, remaining totally secretive about their real activities.

This secretiveness characterizes Gypsy existence in America as elsewhere. It is maintained for the practical purpose of concealing crime, and, even more important, it strengthens the protective wall that the Gypsies insist on keeping between themselves and the non-Gypsies. In a consumer society, and the United States is a prime example, the Gypsies superficially imitate their non-Gypsy enemies. They buy luxury cars and huge color television sets—when possible on credit, and without ever paying for them. Yet they show their contempt for these possessions by battering their cars and letting their expensive television sets fall into disrepair.

The United States, sensitive to the demands of its many ethnic groups and minorities in recent times, has not yet faced the problem of its Gypsy population. It is a special problem. Other minorities want recognition of their cultures and integration without discrimination into American life. But the Gypsies are suspicious and afraid of being corrupted by non-Gypsy societies and do not want to become part of them. They fear, above all, for their children:

100

that contact with non-Gypsies will lead to the disintegration of their traditionally strong family and community ties, and that this will result in juvenile delinquency. They fear that their young people will turn to drugs, to sexual promiscuity, and to large-scale crime.

Nonetheless, the Gypsies—especially the younger ones—are settling down in increasing numbers. There are among them activists who see the gains made by other minority groups and want to share in these gains. They ask for the respect of the non-Gypsy world and for equal job opportunities. The first step, of course, will be education—more than ninety-five percent of the Gypsies in America are illiterate. However, before education is possible, Gypsy parents will have to overcome their fear of corruption by non-Gypsies, and non-Gypsies will have to overcome their long hostility toward and misunderstanding of the Gypsies.

Many other highly complex problems remain. There is the fear that with assimilation many of the Gypsies' traditions and customs will disappear, that a rich culture will be lost. After all, how can a stable society tolerate a group of nomads within its midst without destroying this nomadism? How can Gypsy children, always on the move or wanting to be, attend regular schools? Nomadism, the need to move on, remains fundamental to the Gypsy character. In fact, even those who have settled often paint the ceilings of their rooms blue—to remind them of the open sky; and these rooms, as much as possible, resemble Gypsy caves or tents. When spring comes, Gypsies all over the world feel an irresistible urge to take to the road—even if this means no more than a long spring vacation.

Social scientists have only now begun to study seriously the problems of the Gypsies and the possible solutions to these complex problems. It is to be hoped that they will turn to the Gypsies themselves, a people who have a unique history of adaptability combined with individuality, in finding these solutions. A thorough and sympathetic understanding of these people is certainly a first step in the right direction.

Bibliography and Index

Bibliography

Acton, Thomas. *Gypsy Politics and Social Change*. London and Boston: Routledge & Kegan Paul, 1974.

Borrow, George. *Lavengro*.

———. *The Romany Rye*.

Both of these classic nineteenth-century works are now available in Everyman's Library, published in New York by E. P. Dutton & Co., Inc.

Boswell, Silvester Gordon. *The Book of Boswell: Autobiography of a Gypsy*. London: Victor Gollancz, 1970.

Clébert, Jean-Paul. *The Gypsies*. Translated by Charles Duff. Baltimore: Penguin Books, 1967.

Kenrick, Donald, and Puxon, Grattan. *The Destiny of Europe's Gypsies*. London: Sussex University Press, 1972.

Sandford, Jeremy. *Gypsies*. London: Martin Secker & Warburg Ltd., 1973.

Sutherland, Anne. *Gypsies: The Hidden Americans*. New York: The Free Press, 1975.

Trigg, Elwood B. *Gypsy Demons and Divinities*. Secaucus, N.J.: Citadel Press, 1973.

Vesey-FitzGerald, Brian. *Gypsies of Britain*. Newton Abbot: David & Charles, 1973.

Wedek, H. E. *Dictionary of Gypsy Life and Lore*. New York: Philosophical Library, 1973.

Wood, Manfri Frederick. *In the Life of a Romany Gypsy*. London and Boston: Routledge & Kegan Paul, 1973.

Yoors, Jan. *The Gypsies*. New York: Simon and Schuster, 1967.

Index

Photo Credits

The author wishes to acknowledge for use of photographs:

Les Etudes Tsiganes: 26, 38, 40, 50, 68, 87, 91
Photoworld/FPG: frontispiece, 7, 9, 16, 28, 34–35, 41, 46, 49, 64, 82–83, 88–89, 96, 99
Photos Claquin: 30, 31
Photos Fleury: 43, 44, 59
Photo Marboeuf: 71, 72, 74

About the Author

HOWARD GREENFELD was born and raised in New York City. After attending the University of Chicago and New York University, he earned an M.A. from Columbia University and went to live in Rome, where he taught English. Mr. Greenfeld later returned to New York and worked under Bennett Cerf at Random House, but finding that he missed Italy, he went back, this time to Florence where he began his own publishing house, Orion Press. Under the Orion Imprint, Mr. Greenfeld produced several books, among them an anthology of stories by Hans Christian Andersen, illustrated by children and featured in *Life* magazine. Now living in Italy, Mr. Greenfeld pursues an active career as a writer of books for both children and adults. His recent book for Crown, *Books: From Writer to Reader* received stunning reviews and was chosen for: 1976 ALA Notable Children's Books; 1976 Best Books of the Year, *School Library Journal*; Kirkus Choice; *Horn Book* Fanfare; and the AIGA Book Show.